In the wake
of the
MARY
CELESTE

Gary Crew
&
Robert Ingpen

Lothian
BOOKS

Rose Cottage

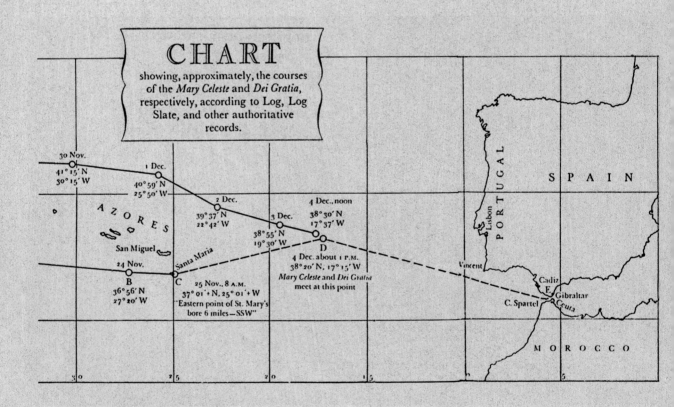

CHART

showing, approximately, the courses of the *Mary Celeste* and *Dei Gratia*, respectively, according to Log, Log Slate, and other authoritative records.

Thomas C. Lothian Pty Ltd
132 Albert Road, South Melbourne, Victoria 3205
www.lothian.com.au

National Library of Australia
Cataloguing-in-Publication data:

Crew, Gary, 1947- .
In the wake of the Mary Celeste.

ISBN 0 7344 0728 9.

1. Mary Celeste (Brig). 2. Shipwrecks - North Atlantic
Ocean - Juvenile fiction. I. Ingpen, Robert, 1936- . II.
Title.

A823.3

Designed by Tina Denham
Pre-press by Digital Imaging Group, Port Melbourne
Printed in China by Everbest Printing

Rose Cottage,
Marion,
Massachussetts.

23rd September, 1903.

For the attention of Mr Arthur Conan Doyle,
Author,

Sir,

While it is a curious coincidence that we share the
same Christian name, I must say from the outset
that I deliberately chose not to use it in addressing
you. Indeed, I only refer to you as 'Sir' according to
the formal courtesies of letter writing. Nor do I use
the term with any reference to your recent knight-
hood. Your being so honoured – and thus placed in
the league of my legendary childhood heroes, the
likes of Sir Galahad and Sir Lancelot – causes me
unimaginable pain. Considering your distinctly
unchivalrous behaviour towards my dear departed
family, I do not think you deserve to be spoken of in
the same breath as those illustrious knights of old.

The Mary Celeste in New York Harbour

You may well turn to the conclusion of this letter to learn who condemns you, for there you will find my name writ clear and bold.

I am Arthur Briggs, the son of Captain Benjamin Spooner Briggs, late Master of the ill-fated brigantine *Mary Celeste*, and his wife, my dear mother, Sarah Elizabeth Briggs.

I am also the brother of Sophia Matilda Briggs, who, along with our parents, died as a result of the tragedy that struck the vessel – although that might mean nothing to you.

Yes, Mr Conan Doyle, it was my family whom you defamed when you wrote so mendaciously of their deaths in your story, 'F. Hakakuk Jephson's Statement', published in the *Cornhill Magazine* of January, 1884.

As if that was not insult enough, you allowed that same story to be published again in 1890, in *The Captain of the Lone Star and Other Stories*.

Arthur Briggs

In those days I was not so bold, but now that I am a man I have the courage to challenge you, Knight of the Realm though you may be. To challenge you not only in words (your own weaponry), but with my bare arm too, or a sword if need be (since a saint's sword comes into my story, as you well know).

And I *would* challenge you physically too, if I were not raised a good Christian like my father, God rest his soul.

But I am beginning to sound as puffed up as yourself, so I will make myself plain and, I hope, put an end to this dreadful business.

Though you may not care to remember, in November 1872, when I was a boy of seven, my father, Captain Briggs, set out from New York in command of the *Mary Celeste*. Aboard was my mother, my two-year-old sister Sophie, and a crew of seven able-bodied seamen. The cargo was 1700 barrels of raw alcohol.

The Mary Celeste *in the Atlantic*

The *Mary Celeste* was bound for Genoa, Italy. She was newly fitted out and an uneventful voyage was expected. Since I was at school I was left at Rose Cottage in the loving care of my grandmother.

I never saw my family again. But that fact is well known to you. To your shame, you took advantage of my loss by fabricating a lie which has grown over the years, until now I can hardly bear to hear of the *Mary Celeste* – or the *Marie Celeste*, as you so transparently renamed her. Still, to my regret, there is hardly a cheap magazine or tawdry Sunday paper where that name is not mentioned.

By what right did you do this?

By what right does any man – and you particularly, being a doctor of medicine and supposedly devoted to healing – by what right, even in the name of literature, does a man take the suffering of another and turn it to his advantage?

As an honest, blunt-speaking Yankee, I find that impossible to understand.

THE BOSTON AGE

"ONLY THE TRUTH"

THE FIFTEENTH OF DECEMBER 1872

LOCAL VESSEL FOUND ADRIFT

PASSENGERS AND CREW MISSING

GIBRALTAR: 15 DECEMBER.
The brigantine *Mary Celeste* of Boston w

Grave fears are held for all who were aboard.

There was no sign of her Captain, Benjamin Spooner Briggs, his wife Sa his two-year o

The vessel was discovered by the crew of the British vessel *Dei Gratia*. She was seaworthy and showed no signs of why her crew may have abandoned her. Crew members of the *Dei Gratia* have to Gibraltar where a

The truth is that the fate of the *Mary Celeste* and all who sailed in her was well known within months of her loss. Until your scurrilous tale was told, there was no mystery, no scandal, no frightful tales of mutiny and murder attributed to those poor unfortunates aboard. The plain facts of the ship being found, adrift and without sign of life, must have been known to you. Heaven knows, the outcome of the Maritime Inquiry conducted in Gibraltar was well enough documented on both sides of the Atlantic.

Simply put, the barrels of alcohol were damaged in a storm, causing the hold to fill with highly flammable fumes. It was obvious, as the Inquiry heard, that out of consideration for the safety of his family and crew, my father gave the order to abandon ship and take to the yawl, which he had towed behind. No doubt he thought that if the fumes did not explode within the hour, the company could reboard the *Mary Celeste* and continue their voyage.

But the tow rope parted, leaving the yawl and her piteous occupants to the mercy of the sea, while the *Mary Celeste*, still under sail, drifted steadily away.

And so my family died.

Dreadful though the story may be, that was the stated belief of the vessel's owner, James H. Winchester. And what reason would he have to lie?

So, I ask, why did you? Why, in the name of all that is Holy, did you concoct the fiction that my mother and sister were thrown overboard? And why did you have my father shot in the face – the *face* – by the same assassin?

It is too cruel.

I see you pause in your reading to shake your head, thinking that I protest too much. If that is so, let me remind you of why I cannot forget. Why I still feel pain. Why, even as an adult, I still grieve for my loved ones, daily …

Arthur and Sophia Briggs

I was just seven years old when this tragedy struck and missed my parents dreadfully, as any child would.

Indeed, I spent my childhood brooding over their deaths. I imagined them dying of thirst in that tiny yawl as it drifted, hopeless, in the Atlantic. I heard my mother's voice as she tried in vain to calm my sister's cries for nourishment. I felt my father's anguish as the dying looked to him to save them.

Yes, although I am older now, those imaginings still remain with me and always will.

But here is the rub.

Though you might not realise it, other writers, possibly not so gifted or famous as yourself , have now clambered aboard this fictional vessel, this *Marie Celeste* which you have created, turning the truth of what happened into a farce of horrific proportions.

I have now read accounts, also purporting to be true, like your own cruel lie, that a giant sea serpent, a legendary Kraken, rose from the deep and attacked my father's vessel, devouring all who were aboard.

Mrs Sarah Briggs with Sophia in the yawl

I have read that my father is still alive, living a life of luxury in some secret corner of the earth, having entered into a shameful financial arrangement with certain charlatans to claim the salvage monies due from the ship that he deliberately abandoned.

I have read that the *Mary Celeste* (or the *Marie Celeste*, since these days so few know the difference between the facts of the matter and your fiction), was attacked by pirates. These brutes purportedly murdered my family (possibly kidnapping my dear sister and selling her into slavery), but were prevented from taking the *Mary Celeste* herself when a rescue vessel appeared on the horizon.

I have read that all aboard drowned when the platform they stood upon fell into the sea as they watched my father (who was supposedly drunk) swim amongst a school of dolphins.

I have even read that all were decapitated by a bloodied sword found in the hold.

Certainly, there was a sword aboard the *Mary Celeste*. This was a ceremonial sword of a type my father collected, with the Cross of Navarre on the hilt. It was as blunt as a brick, and no blood was found upon its blade. That much was made plain at the Maritime Inquiry.

But still the fabrications, in the guise of journalism or literature, continue to grow. And you, Mr Conan Doyle, having begun this cruel fiction, are responsible for that.

Now I would not have you thinking that this letter is written out of some misplaced envy of your literary success. It is not. I am well aware of your skill in creating that wonderful character, Sherlock Holmes, and have frequently enjoyed reading of his exploits.

Thereby hangs the point of this letter. You, better than any other, know that ignorant people contact Scotland Yard regularly and ask that Detective Holmes be assigned to solve some crime or other that has affected their lives. These people foolishly believe that Holmes exists and can help them.

Captain Benjamin Spooner Briggs and his wife, Elizabeth

How is it that you cannot see that these very same people (ignorant though they may be) would also believe the fiction you have created about the loss of the *Mary Celeste*? That they might believe my father was a charlatan, that he and my mother framed an audacious hoax to claim the salvage monies on the vessel?

How is it that you do not reflect upon the gullibility of the person who is so taken in by your cunning craft that he (or she) would believe a lie – no matter how damaging that lie may be?

And so I ask you to consider what you do. To ask yourself, 'What is the responsibility of the writer of fiction? To create, or to fabricate?'

I await your reply.

Yours sincerely,

Arthur Briggs

*Sir Arthur Conan Doyle, author of the Sherlock Holmes detective stories
and the yarn, 'J. Habakuk Jephson's Statement' which began the scandalous
rumours related to the loss of the Mary Celeste*